No Recipe Intended

By Shirley Francis

Copyright © January 13, 2021

© Shirley Francis

A Meredith *Etc* Book

Meredith *Etc*
1052 Maria Court
Jackson, Mississippi 39204-5151
www.meredithetc.com

Published simultaneously in hardback/softcover
Hardcover printed by Kindle Publishing
Softcover printed by Barnes & Noble Press

Trade 6 x 9" Black and White on white paper
ISBN-13: 978-1-7341578-9-5
ISBN-13: 978-1-7341578-8-8

Pages 98 – 15,869 words

No Recipe Intended

By Shirley Francis

https://meredithetc.com/no-recipe-intended/
Make comments on the author's book page

Enjoy 57 poems & seven short stories.

CONTENTS

Chapters° -- Poems°

DEDICATION

This anthology of poems and short stories is dedicated to my Mother Verbie Lee, my sister Jean, my brother Bobby and lastly, to Frankie Joe my best friend ever. May they all Rest in Peace. Good job Y'all! Well done!

ACKNOWLEDGMENTS

I thank my three sons, David, Shannon and Marcus; my oldest grandson, Marcus Christopher and my sisters Charlene, Jessie, and Jean and my niece Vera for all the reassurance they gave me over the years. Many thanks to my friends Melva, Jennifer, Kelly, and Linda and my publisher Meredith. I am amazed amused and very proud to know and have them as friends.

Kelly encouraged me to get my first 10 poems copyrighted. I appreciate Hazel Hall, who has been a friend and confidant for over 30 years. Meredith praised and admired my poetry for over 30 years. She and her late husband Will opened their house and allowed me to write at their kitchen table in 2019; in 2021, I visited, learned and we grew in true sisterhood. Meredith taught me so much in such a short time. I am proud to have her publish my book.

I am very proud to have Jennifer as a friend; she encouraged me with my writing since her teen years. I took my first writing course on her recommendation and loved it. If I had a daughter, I would love her to be modeled after Jennifer.

I am honored for our common friendships and thankful for their place in my life. May God continue to bless and keep them safe and well. I will strive to find new ways to be there for them.

Love Y'all so much!
Shirley Francis

ADVANCE PRAISE for *No Recipe Intended*

This intriguing and thought-provoking collection of poems and short stories by Shirley Francis exposed the good, the bad, and the ugly. She discusses spirituality and lustful and seductive themes without missing a beat. *No Recipe Intended* is a must read for poetry lovers.

William Trest Jr., *Author,*
Reverse Guilty Plea and The New Populist Party

I resonated with Ms. Francis's poems and stories which reminded me of so many people you see growing up in our black communities. Love and hate, shame and pride, and joy and sadness, often share the same bed in our community. Yet, survival is the goal no matter the circumstances. Ms. Francis reminds us to just breath. I will proudly add *No Recipe Intended* on my bookshelf.

Alice W. Beauchamp, *Author, Coach, Storyteller*

By Shirley Francis

THIS BOOK IS PRESENTED TO:

_____

Blog: meredithetc.com

facebook Meredith *Etc*

Meredith*etc*

Join the conversation @
https://meredithetc.com/no-recipe-intended/

ONE

Strength

1970s

Bitter bouts of agony to which I will not succumb,
keep coming back plaguing me,
wonder what I have done.

Can the past be closing in, crowding out the now?
Making the future so unclear,
is this the time to bow?

So turbulent are these rude attacks impossible to ignore.
It is like a magnet pulling me back perhaps just to explore.

Much farther than my past they go at rapid speed it seems
with eyes wide open I now know
the reason for my dreams.

I cannot remember when I was one, two, three, nor four.
But my memories from since then to you
I will place before.

They are not all pleasant and I doubt they ever are.
Many left a wondrous feeling, some a whitened scar.

When sad times befall me now, I rise to see them through
knowing that on the other side is but a different view.

That would not be seen by me if too weak to pay the cost
at the end of each crisis, I am stronger than my loss.

By Shirley Francis

The Winner

When the game is over and the players all tie what
will happen to me grandma will I then die?

Grandma being wise and old already in her grave smiled
down upon him and said, "no, you, I'll save"

Often fear surrounds me and I tremble in fright
Will you come to my bed and comfort me tonight?

Why I have never left your side and I never ever will.
You were standing by me child when time stood still.

Every step you take my dear is not without me.
Why I was sitting next to you up in that chinaberry tree.

Pardon me for laughing but grandma you're so old
to see you climb a chinaberry tree would be a sight to
behold.

There was no effort to it child not a bit on my part
you carried me up that tree right there in your heart.

When you truly love someone and peace with them you find;
they are with you always
in your heart, soul and mind.

The Situation

I want to thank you mother for helping me
in my times of misery.
You stood by me, yes you were right there
Giving every ounce of your tender loving care.

A girl needs her mother at a time like that,
yet some mothers seem to forget.
For me you were like a bridge over troubled waters.
I thank God that I am your daughter.

At times when I was so depressed
There you were with your gentleness.
You gave me support. I held my head high
and smiled at people when I wanted to cry.

Now other people were very nice
They showered me with good advice.
I appreciated their kindness too
But I couldn't have made it without you.

Note:

This poem was written in the summer of 1971 for my mother
Mrs. Verbie Lee Bell who taught me how to take nothing and
make something out of it in no time flat.

By Shirley Francis

Insight

When you leave home and have a baby back there,
although he is with your mother,
people will say you don't care.

But does it really matter to you what they say?
Let them chitter and chatter,
your child will be proud of you someday.

Stick it out it might take a while
just think of the happiness
you will bring to your child.

Yes "you can make it" is something often said
but if you never make an effort
you will never get ahead.

The prize

You are just a baby not even two,
and can't realize how much I love you.

You won't even say hello to mommy on the phone
I guess that's my punishment for not being home.

When I am around you cry, kick, and yell
then look at me like you want to say, "go to hell."

You are a mean little man about whom I boast
because you are the one, I love the most.

You always say no when I say yes
and you think your grandma is the very best.

You have dimples on your cheeks
and one on your chin
I chuckle myself as I watch you grin.

You are the sweetest thing in this whole wide world
you are even sweeter than a baby girl.

You are my heart pride and joy my
precious, precious, baby boy.

By Shirley Francis

Scorned

You are a tiger you are super bad.
You are a man that every woman wish she had.

Your intelligence drives women insane.
You bring them happiness never pain.

The things you do make women feel good.
You, being a superman, I guess they should.
Women say Jim is good, but you are truly better.
How do you feel about this version of yourself fellow?

Now this is what you are to me
a carrier of acute misery.

That intelligence that drives women insane
is nothing but an artificial brain.

The things you do when we are in bed
yes, they make me lose my head.
But then when it comes back to me
reality sinks in and again, I'm free.

So, you don't want anybody to blow your mind
how can they blow something that they can't find?

And your heart is like a piece of grit
Nobody, want it.

You are a big man to be so small super
ego is going to make you fall.
If you don't watch ID.

TWO

The Mother

Bits of Pride

They called you Bit you were so small
So, kind and so unique
Yet no one wondered at all
what you had had to eat.

You strode on though not alone
for God was at your side
and what was wrong you wouldn't condone
still now you have that pride.

Do you remember that cold night
we shivered all together
you prayed to God for some insight
to make our situation better?

You never asked for a weather change,
only wisdom that you might invest.
The knowledge that you have attained
to bring warmth to your nest.

No selfishness could one acquire
from living next to you.
Your goal in life was to inspire
as best as you could do.

Have you done better mother dear
with your sixth-grade education than
parents of the now and here who
dwell on complications?

By Shirley Francis

Recipe

She had a child, and the child was wild.
She said "well I don't know what to say
I don't know how she turned out this way
She rips and runs won't study a bit
I say as her mother that child is unfit.

Every other word is a curse, curse, curse.
Of all my children that one's the worst.
I prayed and prayed hard
Lord you know I did my part.

Don't know what happened along the way
But somehow my child went astray.
She went to Sunday school and to church
Sung in the choir and many hearts she touched.

My child was raised and raised right.
If you say any different you've got a fight!"

Her conscience speaks to her.

"She turned out right just like a cake.
Now she is in the oven getting ready to bake.
And unless something goes right with the temperature
That child of yours is going to burn for sure.

It's not her fault and I don't mean to accuse
But look my dear at the recipe you used.

You had a child put her in a home
from which most of the time you were gone.
You added food clothes shelter at times
in between your whiskies and wines.

No Recipe Intended

You added cruel names, vulgar in nature
Now her ways aggravate you.
You were consistent with your neglect
now you sit and demand respect.

You added lies, humility, and pain
now of her you are ashamed.
You seldom hugged her
Didn't you love her?

I don't pity you and your self-deceit
You didn't add any sugar,
now you want something sweet!"

By Shirley Francis

Conditional Love

Love your father is what the Bible might say
but some folks just don't see it that way.
I talk a lot but it's just because, I want you
to listen to me and hear my point of view.

I never went to school, but I learned how to read and write.
I use to get up early in the morning and read until daylight.
My mother was a wonderful woman as black as the night.
She worked as a slave for my papa you see he was white.

Mama said because he was her master after
she gave birth to me
He said, "Isabel one day soon I'm going to let you and that
child go free."
But that day never came because the old master's wife
had a couple of white men to take mama's life.

I saw mama just before she died.
I fell down on my knees and cried, sighed,
and cried.
That old master didn't even come outside.

I was 13 when they laid my mother in her grave
I loved her so very much that I just couldn't be brave.
Then the master's wife would always beat on me.
I lived in more than slaves, misery,
yet, he would not set me free.

But said he would sale me, his slave
if he was satisfied with the work I gave.
I was 13 when the master's wife passed away
the whole plantation rejoiced that day.

No Recipe Intended

When the master fell on his knees and cried

Not one slave went to his side.
Love your father is what the bible might say
but some folks just don't see it that way.

By Shirley Francis

America

I am hostile you say, and hostile I am.
The reason is because I am overwhelmed.
Scrutiny in the third degree
constantly finding reasons to criticize me.

My self-esteem you attempt to vandalize.
These feelings for you I will not disguise.
No need to greet you with a bright affect.
When I know for me, you are without respect.

No reason to pretend or smile in your face
Your mere existence is a sure disgrace.
Knowing your plot impedes your plan to
separate a nation and destroy a land.

We are building our schools, educating our young
teaching them our story which you have never done.
Their self-discipline and self-esteem are on an incline
you will not be allowed access to their minds.

They will no longer live in a bitter hate state.
We will give them liberty that they may concentrate.
Frustration will no longer in them have a place.
Pride, duty and responsibility will occupy that space.
You put forth an enormous effort
to rob us of life itself.
Deceitfully proclaiming interest in the commonwealth.
Dare you intrude on my parenting skills
my offspring taking everything including my dreams.

There are somethings you just cannot take.

However, since you continue to entrap my children,

I decided to generously give you one of these things.

Here, conspirator take my conscience!

Three

Love

Gratitude

Love to me is no reflex it is brought about by
the bestowment of happiness from one to another.
It is something that should be appreciated if not returned.

When I tell you I love you please don't tell me
that's not a good idea.
Tell me you appreciate it.
If it is a fault?
It is mine and may be a grievous one

Just let me love you for as long as I can
and when the time comes for me to pay and hurt
let me reminisce the peace and pleasure
I found in loving you.

No Recipe Intended

Mister

All I want is a touch of joy, a smile,
a kiss, will do,
a warm caress, your gentleness,
and I will put my trust in you.

I want us to be able to have pleasant conversations.
Most of what we do will be our desires
not just obligations.

I want to make you happy to let you feel how much
I care and not only your smile but your tears too I must share.

I want to stand by and watch as you master your goals.
I want to not only give my heart
but gladly give my soul.

Can you tell I am in love with you
and my feelings refuse to hide?

Can you tell, I am in love with you,
and crave to be by yourside?

By Shirley Francis

Lost

I think of you often I must say
and where I might have been
if you had not come along my unforgotten friend
To me it is known the fact is clear the struggle still I face
No one will ever come along and my time with you erase

For several years you pulled me through
the cracks and crevices.

With goal in mind for me to have the things
I might have missed.

For more than the necessary things the hierarchy we
climbed, the task was clear the search was on a better life
to find.

Your tender touch that meant so much
guidance without control.

Now no one is here my gentle dear to even play your role.

What wouldn't I do to speak to you,
your hand reach out and hold?

Yet, I have been good;
my ground I have stood and done as I was told.

Although summers are not the same
my winters bring no pain.

I walk about day in and out feeling rather strange.
There is a part of me that's gone to not have anymore.
But ah' the memories are mine forever to adore.

The Present

Then God made someone special and said Shirley
This is a special gift for you
We will name him "Lou."

For you can bend him but he will never break.
You can love him with all your mind body, soul, and heart
and never once will you, he forsake.

In time you will grow to honor,
and maybe even cherish him.
He will give you fruit unlike any other
making the whole world applaud.

All you need to do is respect trust and love this, Lou.
He in return will build his world around you.
And Shirley said sadly, "God I don't know how."

God smiled and said, "He will show you."

By Shirley Francis

Four

Serenity

Poise

Thank you, God for many things
for making people like my sister Jean.
Who gives me hope when I do stare in
the face of failure and despair?

For the pleasure for the pain
for the sane and the insane
and those I do not understand
thank you for adding them to your plan.

Thank you for my life as I live it
and may from my experiences I benefit.
My goal in which I constantly seek
is to improve in the areas where I am weak.

Who knows me better than I?
Who can feel the tears that I cry?
Can anyone hear the laughter from my heart?
Does anyone know how it feels to play my part?

Thank you for the educators that you send.
Strengthen my ability to learn from them.
Broaden my insight and judgement please.
Make me more sensitive to others' needs.

Calm

It was not very long ago that I loved that old wormy tree.
For, in my childish state of mind,
I knew it would not leave me.

So, it began the growing did and soon all could see
how tall and beautiful she had grown
yet still a friend to me.

My deepest secrets I did share without reservations,
still this day I do believe
she understood our conversations.

I am sure she felt my tears and the traces of my pain.
But ah' the laughter that we shared was of another reign.

By Shirley Francis

The Driver

If you get in the car on the passenger's side
and are always chauffeured around
you will only be going along for the ride
and can't drive when the chips are down.

So, take control of your life today and
know just where you are going.
Should confusion set in along the way
stop and do some exploring.

Assess the situation,
evaluate the trouble,
get back into the driver's seat
and set your pace on double.

The Fix

While flying through the clouds
so beautiful and bright
my mind begins to float.
I'm with you it's yesternight.

I see myself in a tiny bed not made for two
but darling in my bed there is always room for you.

The clouds are nice and fluffy,
and I feel so secure.
Your arms are so engulfing.
Our love is surely pure.

"Pure what?" Says the girl who loves him even more.
You will fill his life with agony,
you have done it once before!"
The clouds are turning gray now the rain is about to come.
Shut up you little paragon and let me have my fun!

But she is so determined to put me to disgrace.
The paragon walks up to me and slaps me in my face.
The clouds are dark and loathsome
Apprehension everywhere.

She yells out, "I love him, don't you even care?"
I say to her, "You silly fool don't you understand it
doesn't matter at all to me take him if you can.
Go over and hold his hand."

She goes to him and says to him, "I love you so my dear."
He looks at her and says to her, "Girl get away from here!"
She looks at me I feel her pain, her shame her agony.
I laugh at her I do not hide I do this boldly.
Then say to her, "crack is not bad just try and you will see."

Composure

Today a storm came over me that I slowly overcame.
Still when the calm had crept right in,
I felt the intense pain.

The anger that had rendered in fulfilled my blood shot eyes,
and all the people loved by me were suddenly despised.

How cruel at first it felt of me
to judge their every move.
Who was I to sit and critique or even disapprove?
I watched them as they laughed
and heard them as they spoke.
Yet all the while it seemed like just a nauseating joke.

So hard my efforts were to be a social part of this
But all the while my teeth were clinched
and tightly balled my fists.

The day did not leave nor did they, so we were left alone
Only God felt my pain as I sat right there and moaned.

There was no effort made by me to offer up a prayer.
Perhaps, I had convinced myself that God just did not care.

If you think that things got better,
well, they weren't expected to.

A situation will not just change
if one does not know what to do.

So, I went into the bathroom to try and cry a bit
then suddenly my stomach cramped and so I emptied it.

Five
Odd

The Affair

The sun was lit the earth smelt of it
Yet the moon refused to dance
she dared to take a chance.
Still, we lingered on for we were not strong
Are we ever strong when we are wrong?

Yet I lived for you as you lived for me.
We never once thought about integrity.
Our bodies ached when we were apart.
We stayed together to spare our hearts.

The ducks were so grand and the water so great.
The waves stilled themselves to anticipate
for they too were curious of our fate.
Our hearts we did nothing to aggravate.

And we swam the sea just you and me,
and went over it thrice again
to prove we were more than friends.

You held my hands you kissed my lips
and gently caressed my breast.

I trembled in fear to my husband dear
I humbly ran and confessed.
Still, I had no shame though my loss was no gain.

By Shirley Francis

His sorry and pain nearly drove me insane.

Yet I did it again and again this happens when
one becomes vain.

A new heart I would have to obtain.

Should we just stop, and the pleasure drop
and go on our merry way.

For certain we would have to pay
if not tomorrow some later day.
Your wife does she know that you love me "too much"
that I tremble when we meet before we even touch.

Will she someday have sorrowing pain
and you not be ashamed?
Will she hurt cry and wish to die
when you are out here with me?
When you go home after we have been alone
can you look at her lovingly?

Can you hold her hands kiss her lips,
and gently caress her breast?

What is love what is lust,
what is respect and trust,
can you guess?

Kinky

A craving that never possessed me
soared smoothly through my entirety
causing my face to flush body to jerk
lips to part with perhaps a little smirk.

Seizure like movement perfect ecstasy
newly found pleasure forgotten agony
diaphragm muscles began to contract
Heartbeat so rapid I could not relax.

Timid eyes that had known only shyness
now danced around enjoying the bliss.
Screaming confusion cried how did this start
Lust stimulated every beat of my heart.

Each breath I took was like a gentle flight
Through the pale brown clouds of this yesternight.
This must be the feeling of cocaine
But no raw substance has entered my veins.
She caressed and engulfed my breast;
my rebuttal to her was non the less
A soft warm scent saturated the air
as I rubbed her short brown kinky hair.

Her ebony skin was smoother than silk
Soon I enfolded her in a warm quilt.
Bad I can no longer afford to be
I must please my husband and society.

By Shirley Francis

The Process

She was just a child one must recall
when selling for a quarter
who would believe she would someday
grieve the mother of this daughter?

Tall, thin, and brown with lips so round
Precious she was called
eyes like a snake lust as her bait
she vowed to make men crawl.

There was no plan to prove her sane
some certainly knew her secrete.
Was it her plan to have no shame
or did Precious just postpone it?

Throughout the world this pretty girl
did what, got her want
while deep inside her tarnished pride
screamed don't Precious don't.

To comprehend my little friend
you must travel in her shoes.
To understand is hard for men
who have never been abused.

Precious's mother could not do a thing
As her life was absorbed in agony and pain.
This little girl she knew so well
would spend her life in a padded cell.

Do you Know?

Some folks think it is wrong
'cause society still have slaves.
Others think it is wrong because babes are having babes.

Can you have freedom if you don't have education.
Were babes not having babes at the start of this creation?

I don't know.

A woman said to me you better leave that man alone.
He still has a wife and you a husband at home.

Open your eyes girl you are looking mighty blind.
A married woman ought not be
a married man's concubine.

I don't know.

Complaints are being made about the way things are.
He rides the bus while his sister drives a car.

Both were raised in the same house during the same time.
He jumped for the penny while she jumped for the dime.

I don't know.

Nodding

Excuse me if I am paranoid excuse me if you, please
because when you teach your history,
it causes this disease.

My definition of mister when it comes from your demand
is listen, idiot listen, and I hope you will understand.

Sometimes I must patronize you just to keep my job.
You give others liberty to rape kill and rob.

Now your crack cocaine is killing off my kin.
Do you think I should be kind to you,
or seek to be your friend?

Listen, mister, listen, and I hope you understand
I am calling you mister
and it comes from your demand.

No Recipe Intended

Prophecy

It matters not how you see me
not one bit.

Just remember as you watch me
what you see, is what you get.

When you see me today,
don't slap your face
and say darn it.

Remember the self-fulfilling prophecy
and not think of me as an itch.

By Shirley Francis

Hills and Valleys

Sometimes life is cruel to me
It's not what I thought it would be
So, I wonder.

My love was given because I prioritized.
Were the decisions made by me not wise?
I just wonder.

Now because my best was done
and I'm getting old but not having fun.
I wonder.

There is no sunshine just rain and thunder.
It is hard to bow down and be humble.
So, I wonder.
Then, I smile and find that happy place.
The one that time could not erase.

My motherly years when I laughed a lot
as I kissed their heads as I wiped their snot...
I stopped wondering.

I am thankful for all the simple things
and all the joy that life brings
The good the bad the ugly too.

I would do it all over if I had to.
I smile. I am a part of you.
I don't wonder.

I'm proud, blessed, and humble.

Tears

I cry tears in the day as I sit on my bed.
Tears to the heaven way up above.
Tears to the people down here below.
Some are my friends; some are my foes.

Tears stream down my face, yes, I cry a lot.
Mostly, happy tears are the ones that I have got.
Tears and a chuckle are what I offer you.
My love hugs and kisses are given freely too.

Memories are what I make as I go on my merry way.
Tears are supposed to be shared
to enhance our special day.

By Shirley Francis

Six

Found

Taken

You do what you must do.
I hope you want to do what you have to do.

But do you keep me off your mind
or do you try and keep on trying.

You are with me most of the time
Somehow life has made you mine.

Is it something that you have done
were you love or just fun?
Answer two or answer none.

Marching on without a fight.
Our behavior was not right.

We stopped to eat some forbidden fruit.
Paid the price for our chosen route

The punishment is as it should be.
A smile is just a curtesy not an apology.

Let us admit the problem confess our wrong
make it right and let life go on.

Wonder

I get comfort in having you in my heart
my lips smile when I think of you and your gentleness.
You are not here to kiss and caress me
but have left great memories.
You have always been there for me
I feel your love everyday
this is pleasing.

Your awareness and sense of humor
doesn't hurt the situation either.

I know it is selfish and prejudice but if I could make
a carbon copy of anyone, it would be you.

I am trying to let you know how much you mean to me.
Sometimes words cannot convey what the heart feels.

Enough

I am tired, just so tired, of these misunderstandings
people seem to have of me.
I just want to live in a great society based on
fairness and equal opportunity.
I am tired of the ways of the world
and fear the next tragedy.
Can't you see, use the key, set us free, set us free!

I am tired of walking on my tip toes
and running around checking my doors.
There are children living somewhere near you
that may not have food or clothes.
I am tired of our public servants getting richer
and richer each day.
While we shuffle, scuffle, and hustle
and still our bills we can barely pay.

When did public servants start making so much money?
This is pathetic but the fat cats seem to think it is funny.
Who can relieve my fears
by making this situation disappear?

Congressmen over 500 of them they each make over
$170,000 per year.
I'm so tired of these unnecessary killings
of people of the colored race.

Can you remember when a policeman would stop you
if you ran, he would be up for the chase?
Now our public servants who we trust
are killing many of us.

Let's make a fuss how can we trust those

who are abusing us.

We used to be afraid of the billy club, then, the taser gun.
But now they don't have to chase us
because we are afraid to run.
From the moment they stop us they reach
and pull out their gun.

They never aim for the legs or the arms
they claim they fear us as they pick us off one by one.

Seldom is anything ever done.
Old people eating their pet's food
and hungry children wishing for some.
How come, how come, how come?

I'm so very tired of learning lies
about you and me
which is taught to us
in white supremist history.

Still, we walk around like we cannot even see.
Oftentimes in agony oppression
leads to misery.

Knowledge is the master key; set us free; set us free.
Give up your white supremacy, can't you see?
Recession hurts you as well as me, can't you see?
So just give up your white supremacy,
can't you see?

I am tired of old people creating wars for young
people to go out and fight.
You know that this is not right.
Don't see how they can sleep at night.
But they don't even seem uptight.

By Shirley Francis

They can use the money that we pay
them to go out and buy a smile
All the while, All the while
A mother screams out not my child,
please, not my child.

The public servant claims your child
died protecting you.
He did what he was supposed to do.
The mother screamed out, "protecting who?"
That is something you older ones should do.

Let us see how eager you would be to fight
you would not make a decision overnight.
If the battle you had to go and fight,
you would think of reasons why it was not right.

No Recipe Intended

To Swen

Love, I hope you had a great start
to your week and all is well.

Thank you for allowing me
to spend time with you
last week.

It is always a great pleasure to be in your company – to hear
you express yourself and explore your thoughts and feelings
and hear all the wisdom come out that beautiful head.

I love just sitting watching you move around
watching your eyes glistening
and your mouth go from pouty to a smirk
then back to soft pouty lips to a laugh.
Thanks for always being there.

To Him

Good afternoon I hope you are having a great day.
You are so welcome thank you for being
an important part of my life
and letting me into your world.

I will always treasure the wonderful memories
of time spent loving you.

Today, I miss you, really miss you
sacrifice is no stranger to me.

I am a part of the scene I know the predicament we are in.
Thank you for always being there for me
I am grateful you are a friend and a confidant.
May peace, love, joy, and happiness
always be around to embrace you.

The Note

Hello pretty lady.
I'm upstairs getting rid of a ton of papers etc.
and wondering how you are
and what you are doing
I am so proud
happy and fortunate to have been loved
and shared love with you.
Never in my life have I ever enjoyed
and cherished the fun.
Intimacy and precious relationship
only few will ever experience…
Thank you
Are you up?

By Shirley Francis

Trust

When the story is over and reality kicks in
Can I count on you to be a loyal friend?

Can I depend on you from the beginning to the end?
Or are you standing by me
for yourself when you need to be?

Are you honest and open
and have my best interest in clear view?
Is it worthy of my time to place my confidence in you?

Can I get your take on this?
Please give your point of view.

SEVEN
GUILTY

Life

I don't know what makes me write things
straight from my heart.
But what I know is I ache when we are apart.
It is not the type of pain that maims or kills if you will.
Just the type that moves right on
while time is standing still.

Enough to make me shiver
from the thought that you are gone.
That I will wake up and find my dear
I am on my own.
Nightmare is such a gentle word to use for this situation.
While I in anguish somewhere sit filled with frustrations.

Without surprise I will face the fire flames
just burning through.
While remembering each stolen moment
stolen to be with you.
Still no regret will I succumb
for there is simply room for none.
No damage was there ever done
the game was played, we had our fun,

So, simple were the rules, you see
I would not hurt you; you would not hurt me.
Now somehow pain is creeping in
and I have lost that saintly grin
I am not prepared to just be your friend

By Shirley Francis

I did not see it coming,
but now it must end.

Jean

I won't even stop to wonder
what I would do without you in my life
for you have been with me through my
pleasure and my strife.

The one who has been my backbone
though mother said I only had a gristle.
You have been my torpedo when I needed a missile.

You have been my teddy bear
when I needed a great big hug.
And when I needed a spiritual bath
it was you who provided the tub.

And when I would get so ugly, I could not stand myself
you gently squeezed it out of me until none was left.

Remember the time old Skinky chased me up that tree?
What made it even worse he through dirt balls at me.

Because I could not duck, he landed one in each eye
It felt like the pain from a hammer.
I could not even cry.

You grabbed that joker by his neck
and choked him to the ground.
There I sat afraid of heights
and could not come down.

You were too afraid of heights
You crossed your legs
and scratched your head
then ran into our house.

By Shirley Francis

Then, you returned and kicked Skinky twice
then called him a stinky louse.

Then I heard the chopping of an axe on that tree.
But ah I was never ever for one moment afraid
for I knew you would catch me before I hit my head.

And you did and you still do
And I will always love you!

Glory

Now something pleasant I must write for
God permitting such a perfect night.

My children are happy, healthy, and wise
This is felt as I look in their eyes.

They speak of no evil as they think not the such;
their kisses good night to me mean so much.

There is one far away but deep in my heart.
I am housing him there in a special part.

I am armed with love, honesty, and truth
though aging in years I cling to my youth.

Which might I remind myself was not without pain
but overcoming obstacles is life's toughest game.

The struggle is still on and it will not end.
Life must be caressed every now and again.

She is somewhat like a baby if you know what I mean
Things are more pleasant when her diaper is clean.

This was all said for you not to forget.
You cannot get through life if you are so full of it.

By Shirley Francis

Vows

Well, I know he loves me and always has.
He said it was built out of steel - not out of glass.

For many years we have been married
me being the center of his life
of all the women he chose me to be his wife.

Our children are grown and gone. Finally,
I thought he was mine all alone.

His kisses are more passionate, yet so few.
Still, he makes my body feel like it needs to.

But 16 hours a day we are apart.
I often ask myself when did this start.

All his time with me is being robbed.
Can't he see there is no need for a part-time job.

Today I saw my godchild my babysitter's daughter.
Took a closer look because something was out of order.

I had seen her once a week for more than 20 years
Looking at her now gave me hot flashes and chills.

As she spoke, I shuddered and then came that smile.
Seemed like I was looking into the face of my own child.

Her eyes were like my husbands, nose and cheeks too
When I saw that gap between her teeth, I knew it was true.
This precious angel who called me god mommy dear
had opened my eyes but left my heart full of fear.

For a week now I have followed him to his part-time job.

I know for a fact that I am being robbed.

I'm just sitting and giving and wasting it away.
The dog has gone astray now so the cat must play.
I've decided to be faithful to myself
and get a full-time life.
He can keep his part-time job.
I will be his part-time wife.

Touching

You are such a touching person one whom I admire.
You have a beautiful personality
and are so eager to inspire.

You had a problem and came to me,
I opened my ears to hear.
Then shared your problem with love and sympathy

From my heart there came a tear
It is not unusual but heartbreaking for
you this is not fair.

The thought to me is breathtaking
you are thrown into the hands,
of a mind who does not care.

So full of sympathy and feeling close to you.
I let you embrace me not thinking of what it might lead to.

You are so precious loved one,
with inner beauty so divine.
I hate to see anyone toying with your mind.

I cannot get involved.
I am too close to your wife.
I pray that your problems will be solved and
that you will have a much happier life.

Who

I think of you because I must
a drive of passion pleasure and lust.

Your body moves me.
I cannot leave you behind.
My daydreams are focused with you in mind.

A trembling chill goes down my spine
perhaps a thrill some never find
written words just to say
you are the start of my morning
and the end of my day.

By Shirley Francis

Eight
The Chosen

Chosen

People do things for different reasons
That is probably why God made different seasons
My friend girl had a season of joy and bliss
while I experienced none of this.

God made more than one season and he
rotated them for you and me.
Pray when will your season come,
pray when will it be?
Is probably often, to God your plea.
I did that and my season came to me.

But not before I experienced many years of misery
and I'm still not happy, joyous, and free.
I just get up and feel like I am in the winter stage
Do what I do and turn the page.

A good season does not jump up and down
and say look I am here.
You must remember the past my dear.
Perhaps your season has not come.
There are things you can do to help it along.

Remember the seasons how many are they?
Don't sit around and let yours slip away.
Get up tiger and get on your knees
and say to God pretty please.
He understands all our needs.

No Recipe Intended

If you miss one season there will be another.
So, prepare yourself and avoid the trouble.

God has a sense of humor you know.
And He laughs out loud as he watches us grow.

But God cries when we stand still you know.

So, get on the ball and let his rod and staff comfort you.
Let God be a part of all you do.
If you are not working your life
and your season is here
my condolence goes out to you my dear.

If you are doing your best
and that is the best you can do
and still your life is not working for you,
you might want to give a shout out to you know who.
He has a wonderful sense of humor you know.

Oh yes, the Bible is full of good info.

By Shirley Francis

Haiku

The circle widens.

Volcanic eruption pain

No woman. No man.

<u>Haiku</u>

Bags deflate and fold

Sloughing stridor flaming pain

Rolled up thin control.

By Shirley Francis

Fun

Battered Bastards

Kitty cat scratched a batch of battered bastards.

A batch of battered bastards,
kitty cat scratched.

If kitty cat scratched
a batch of battered bastards

Where is the batch of battered bastards
kitty cat
scratched?

Beloved

I went away and left you there
would I do that again?
You were just a baby then
and did not know my name.
I made the greatest sacrifice,
and it was not in vain.
All the while I felt alone
my purpose oh' so strange.

But there was something deep within
that somehow eased the pain.
I was so bold I claimed my goal that
helped me struggle through.
My dream was of wonderful things
we would someday do
yet, how there was no clue.

I pondered on my darling son someday
I would be with you.
Life was rough and we were tough we
knew we would make it through.
Up the ladder why should it matter the
goal was for me and you.
Would we climb high and reach the sky
who knew what we would do?

Accomplished my plan little man
then I came back for you.
Though it was tough we called life's bluff,
and prayed and our dreams came true.
Years went by we reached the sky
you always pulled me through,
I am so thankful for you.

Triumph

He went to school and learned the skill
to choose his words to fit his will.

Along the way he learned the trait
to use himself as sucker bait.

He used charisma in my point of view
to get people to do what he wanted them to.

Do not mistake him for being just cleaver
for my friend was on a much higher level.

He could make the saddest person laugh
and with that same tongue cut the happiest one in half.

He was a genius the world would someday know
I hope to be smiling when I say
I told you so.

He has had fortune
and a slight taste of fame
also been slandered
and put to shame.

He has fumbled stumbled and tumbled
jumped back up shook it all off
took a deep breath
and not once has he crumbled.

Mighty fine

Someday you might encounter an obstacle
which you feel you cannot climb.
Remember it is just a trial or tribulation
think and you will do just find
often in the nick of time.

Yesteryear was tough and nearly overwhelmed you.
Today you can scream out it is a done deal
be proud you made it through.
The days will often be harder
while waiting for your tomorrow.

Let us toast for the determination within you for true.
You may scream cry and yell,
experience life's days filled with hell.
They tend to amaze not amuse you
how life's days can abuse you.

You will be just fine tomorrow
if you can shake off yesterday's sorrows.
Come on shake them off stand tall
you just stumbled; you did not fall.
Seize the journey make it an adventure.

Use everything yesteryears put in you
that is how you do it
that is how you beat the game
don't you know?
Just grow!

NINE

Edgy Short Stories

Astonished

She woke up one morning and cried out, "where is my husband?" She could not find him anywhere. She looked and she looked, and she looked but still could not find him. So, she went to church seven Sundays in a row and still no husband was found.

Then she cried out, "God where is my husband?"

She heard a voice – He got killed in the war long over two decades ago – No! she screamed out and stomped her foot on the floor. He was killed while resting in his mother's womb - a fortune teller told her. No! she said and kept right on looking for him. He has been in jail for over 27 years for sexual harassment and battery on a policewoman a friend of hers told her. Say it ain't so. Lord please say it ain't so! She pleaded.

Someone said no he has been in the crazy house for at least that long. He was a homosexual and left you for your neighbor's husband they joined the navy and are somewhere on a ship now; but where am I and my children now? You are in a mental institution and your children are grown and gone now.

They blamed you for everything - No! Where is my husband? Lord say it ain't so! Just say it ain't so! She screamed out. He is on crack, and you know who is happy about it as usual - it is Pinkie. A church member told her. Are you sure? Are you positive?! No, she is a liar from the pit of hell I tell you. He is on heroin and in purgatory.

That should make you happy. Please Lord just say it ain'tso, say it ain't so!

Was he white? she asked the crowd in her mind – and they laughed so hard she was only comforted by her husband.

Eve

She sat out on the pool deck underneath the canopy staring at the crystal lake. Sun continuously beaming down on her soft brown skin as if it felt she needed a tan. More than 300 shoestring plaits draped themselves around her shoulders and rested on her breast, the same breast that fed three children yet never lost its firmness nor sensitivity to the gentle stroke of a hand, tongue, or lips.

A serene like smile came over her, felt throughout her blushing body, as she secretly thought of that forbidden fruit she nibbled at a time or two. A craving unlike any that had ever possessed her soared through her entirety causing her face to blush, and body to jerk in seizure like movement. The muscles in her diaphragm contracted while eyes that had never known shyness became timid as those erotic veins that had never been injected with raw material became so filled and stimulate with every beat of her heart and each breath she took was a gentle flight through the pale brown clouds of a fulfilled fantasy.

She leaned back stretching her arms out, eyes closed.   Her husband approached her, kissed her on her lips and asked, "Darling what were you thinking with that sparkling look on your face?" His 6'1" 190 lb. frame stood over her close enough for her to appreciate his emerald, green eyes and blonde streaked hair.

"Of how much I love you and how happy and honest you've made me," she said, smiling into his eyes, thinking and how happy I will be when you take your ass to work so, I can get another nibble from that forbidden fruit.

"And what have I done lately to make you so happy, honest and full of love?" Let's see the little lying hussy answer this with a straight face he chuckled to himself.

What in the hell made him ask me that? She thought, feeling uneasy knowing he expected a well composed convincing lie.

"Darling why would you even ask? Have you not been a great father, husband, lover and friend?" She responded, with deeper fillings screaming out, now is yourchance to evaluate the situation and perhaps d i s c o v e r your own inadequacies. Yes, yes, a great father you are, but husband lover and friend, now analyze this yourself and then figure out the basis of my peaceful thoughts, if you can?

"If this is all so Precious, then why are you caring around condoms in your purse?" Squirm baby squirm he thought, looking at her as if his pleading eyes really needed an explanation.

"You're not being unfaithful to me, are you?" I mean you are not letting someone else mess with my fruit, are you?' Angrily thinking to himself, and not allowing me to watch coach and enjoy.

"Why would you think that?

How could you even fix your mouth to say a thing like that? Don't you trust me anymore?" She very dramatically interjected cunningly looking up at him as he stood arms folded rocking looking down on her knowing that she knew he had somehow peeped her hold card. As quiet as it's kept, she thought, even if he knows he really can't do a darn thing about it. After all it was his idea in the first place to let me have a bite of the forbidden fruit.

"Please honey," he had said, "All you need to do is just flirt with him a little, lead him on I'll act like I'm asleep, then you seduce him. When everything is hot and heavy, I'll come over and reassure him that everything is okay, and we'll all have some fun. Just do it this one time for me. If you don't like it. I promise you will never be asked to do it again."

The fact was she did like it but even more so when she could select her prey and then find herself captured by the game, away from her husband and able to scream out in sheer ecstasy as loud as she wanted to. She smiled up at her husband leaned over and kissed him seductively marveling at her skill.

Secretly thinking to herself, "Condoms, lord I hope he doesn't go near the footlocker, goodness is it ever packed."

Fastbreak

"Get out of those beds, get out of those damned beds now," she yelled, looking like a wild heathen. Her hair sticking up on her head with eyes stretched as if Leonardo had painted them like that.

"Ya'll just stay in those rooms," screamed Steven, "um go eat all of this breakfast before it gets cold, ain't no use in letting grits, eggs and bacon ruin. Um, countin' to five and if ya'll ain't out here it's all mine."

"I'll put my mama flapping foot up your ass if you touch my food," yelled Sarah, approaching the table wearing only a bra and drawers.

The heathen looking woman continued to beat on the doors to wake her peers for breakfast. When she opened the door to room 103, he was covered only by a sheet with rapid hand movement from his midsection.

"Just a minute," he smiled, "I'm coming…"

"You nasty buzzard," she shouted, slamming the door in amazement.

"Baby doll come out of that bathroom right now and get to that table. I'm getting tired of watching you brush your gums every morning like a fool, a poor little fool.

"Watch your mouth," Baby doll said – head twisted to the side showing bare gum, "cause God done promised me if I brush my gums for 328 days three times a day, he will give me a new set of teeth and I respects Him for it. Where are those lazy ass nurses with our coffee?

Miss Perception

The people in the white uniforms used keys to enter or exit the unit. They were separated from the unit by a 1 0 x 1 1 station, enclosed from the floor up by 4 ft. of paneling, encased in glass from there to the ceiling the walls of the unit were of a soft yellow hue enhanced by nicely arranged graffiti.

The locked part of the unit contained eight rooms in an L shape. An extended corridor with a male and female latrine at the far end separated the rooms from a day room with a table, 10 chairs, a TV, and several tables and magazines. A woman came out of room 103, entered the open area, sat by the TV hit it on each side two strong blows then looked back toward the station and yelled out, "how do you make it work? What's the password?"

A middle-aged, blonde-haired woman opened the door at the station and said, "Julie, I'm tired of telling you the same thing over and over. You know how to get the TV turned on, don't you?"

Oh yeah that's right the nurses at the station have to turn it on. "Very good, pretty soon you'll be going out front on the open unit. I'm proud of you Julie." The nurse gave praise.

"Well bitch! that's mighty white of you; it ain't like we don't have good sense. Ya'll white folks just think us colored folks all crazy and shit, but I got news for yo' ass..."

"Now that's enough, Julie that's just enough I will not listen to your nonsense. What color are you?"

"I'm black, and I'm proud of it."

"No, no that's a part of your illness making you think like that

– a delusion. You are a 22-year-old blonde haired white woman."

Julie falls back in her seat and starts laughing out loud, "you're fucking with me now, you're really fucking with me now."

Then she started crying, "Why are ya'll trying to drive me crazy? Why, just why?"

"We are not trying to drive you crazy Julie. I'm a nurse; you are a mental patient on a psychiatric unit suffering from a delusional disorder. We are trying to help orient you to reality. Now come with me to the bathroom and we will just have a look in the mirror and let you see for yourself that you are of Caucasian decent and as white as I am."

"Okay, Okay. I believe you." She responded.

The nurse goes back into the station. Julie flops down in one of the chairs turns her head away from the station and says, "lying bitch."

A tall young well statured man came from room 107. Julie rushed him as he sat down in front of the TV. She then sat across from him, staring him up and down.

"I like to watch TV. Do you like to watch TV?" She asked.

"My name is Julie. What's your name?"

"Al, as in Alphonso." He whispered.

"What you in for murder or rape?" she asked.

"Um just in here to get me some medication, a place to stay and my SSI check started back up. Ain't nothing wrong with me. I just keep coming back to these crazy houses to keep getting the benefits. You know?"

He made eye contact with her, opened his legs, held his penis inside his pants, leaned forward toward Julie and said, there are a lot of benefits in here, you know."

She jumped up, pulled her dress over her head, threw it to the floor and walked toward him saying, "I like to fuck. Do you like to fuck? Cause you can fuck me. I don't care if you're white. Cause I've fucked white men before, yeah I've had syphilis, gonorrhea and crabs."

The nurse and two men came running from the station. She instructed Julie to pick up her clothes and go into her room and put them on.

Julie went into room 109. The nurse immediately went in behind her. They both came back out and the nurse led her into room 103.

A fat middle aged bald man came flying out of room 109 with his penis in his hand, looked up and down the corridor, then rushed into the day room and asked, "where did the naked woman go? Can she take it in the mouth?" The two men who had come out of the station quickly escorted him back into room 109.

A loud buzzer sounded. "Will one of you let the visitors in? I'm in here helping Julie dress," the nurse yelled. One of the men from the station went out and returned with a heavy set elderly dark skinned black man and a very fair skinned, freckled faced, black woman.

"We are here to see Julie," the woman stated.

"Have a seat and she will be out in a minute," the man from the station said. Then yelled," Nancy, Julie has visitors.

Nancy entered the day area from Julie's room. She went over to the couple and said, "Thank goodness she has friends, you people are so supportive of her, and God knows the child needs support. She is so sick and confused and her family never shows up. Not one of them. Not one day in two weeks."

The woman stands up and says, "excuse me," looking the nurse in the face. "We have been here every day. I'm her mother and this is her father. Just what do you mean by her family never shows up?

How sick is my baby?

Will someone please talk to us?"

Portrait of a Paragon

She awakened. Without the aid of a caress from the gentle stroke of a lover, nor the beaming, sun shining through her window, or even the crowing sound made by a well-fed rooster. Her awakening was abrupt. She squirmed about in bed like a frightened little girl, maintaining the fetal position, slowly opening her eyes to the erratic call of her future. Love and joy baffled her.

"What's causing these anxiety attacks," she asked herself.

"Why am I so petrified? What is there to fear? Am I not happy to be free and doing what I want to do?"

Immediately her inner being launched the truth at her. Ah you fear yourself and your own inadequacies. You know full well that you are not prepared to take that advanced cardiac life support course today. How could you be when not once have you even opened the book. Poor little fool, trifling as hell.

Shut up, she thought jumping out of bed. Subconsciously praying to find a reason to cancel the 9am scheduled course. The sound of rain beating down against the window lured her over to the door which she opened and stood unfocused, blank not even aware of her surroundings. The rain subsided and she attempted to close the door which was jammed.

I'll be late. I can't afford to be late not to this! The maintenance man would not be in before 9am. I'll have to cancel, she thought, with feelings of ambivalence, then joy. Maybe there is a bright side to this day after all. Maybe it will be the best day of my life she chuckled.

The phone rang. It was her lover. The man whom she had

moved so far away from to dissolve their relationship. Excitement soared through her as she hung up the phone exclaiming, "Yes, yes, today is all mine! No work, no class, just my man, my pleasure, my day."

Of course, he would have to make the 153-mile three- hour drive, but that would give her all the time she needed to make herself her sexiest. A pedicure, a manicure, a shampoo and set but of course he would repay her for it all when he arrived.

How foolish was she to think she could move away from six years of life, deserting compassion, intimacy, and friendship?

Three hours later the phone rang. The feeling of euphoria embraced her. She elegantly strutted to her car like a self-assured paragon. Her diamond ring sparking on her left index finger as if it were a baby drop of sunshine. While herhead was midair reality slapped her face a stroke or two and she quickly came to herself.

"Oh, I must take this ring off. Don't want him to think I'm a showoff or know how much I truly love this ring."

After the ring was safely placed in its box and planted in the back of the bedroom closet, she ventured to Walmart to meet her lover and bring him back to her apartment.

There he is! There he is! She thought. Walking closer to him she noted not excitement but a somewhat drained look about him which she attributed to his 66 years, the three-hour drive, and the two months of longing for her during their separation. She embraced him with feelings of certainty that everything would be just fine as soon as theygot back to the apartment and he was able to exhale, have a drink or two, sit relax, and hold her for a while.

When they entered the apartment, she hugged and kissed him. He still seemed preoccupied. There was a knock at the door. She stopped kissing him and quickly answered it to find a tall pale firmly built white woman there. She politely told the woman she must have the wrong house and safely closed the door. Two more knocks and in the mist of him saying, "darling, darling," she quickly reopened the door thinking it was a solicitor and briskly asked, "may I help you?"

The woman replied, "I'm Judith his wife."

Amazed and shocked she attempted to close the door; then, she trembled managing to say no to his wife's requests to enter her house.

"I promise not to hurt you, "the woman assured her. "I just need to talk, please."

"Please baby," the man finally whispered. "She won't hurt you. She must talk to you. I had to bring her. Please let her in."

"No," she screamed. "Hell no. Why? Why would you do this? I cannot take it."

"Get away from me, "she snarled, pulling back from him wounded by shame.

Anxiety, embarrassment, humiliation and fear engulfed her. She felt naked, trapped, betrayed, uncontrollably astonished. He approached and embraced her with tenderness reassuring her this had to be done. With eyes closed, she stood limply rocking in his arms striving to regain her composure.

Finally she yelled, "Okay, okay, through the closed door – "first I must search your coat and purse."

Judith agreed to being searched and reassured her that she meant her no physical harm. The door was slowly opened. The search was done.

"So, you are Evangeline," Judith said, as calmly as the circumstances would allow.

"Yes, yes, yes," Evangeline nervously responded pacing about wringing her hands closely observing her surroundings.

"Wait one minute before we do anything. I need to call my friend and she can be over here in a matter of minutes, if necessary," she threatened.

Quickly the phone call was made, and the situation was explained. The conversation started and was interrupted again.

"Wait, wait, I'm nervous. I must call my sister. I must let her know what is happening, that you are both here in my apartment in case something happens to me. The call was made and again the conversation started.

"Wait, wait I can't do this!" Evangeline screamed out, shaking her hands in the air, "I'm just too nervous. I can't calm down."

"I have some klonopin, pills the doctor gave me for my nerves," Judith said.

"No, no, I know what she needs," The man responded."I'll just go up to the store and get her some beer that will calm her down. Right baby?" He said looking at Evangeline, who was looking at his wife.

"You give me the klonopin and you go get the beer," She sneered, still trembling.

By Shirley Francis

The journey through the next three hours was filled with accusa-
tions and frustrations, like magnets set a post to pull each ounce
of remorse embedded in Evangeline's soul. Astonishment again
filled the air as Evangeline inhaled and exhaled, looking Judith
in her tear-filled eyes exclaimed "I'm sorry but only for the pain
you suffer as a result of my relationship with your husband."

Of the moments we spent together, I have no sorrow to offer
and especially for this predicament I cannot apologize for this.
She walked over to the man and held his cheeks in her hands
looking him in his eyes; she spoke in a calm well composed voice
saying, "he has loved me softly and taught me how to respond to
such love, the art of assertiveness, how to love myself and the
world congruently."

I at the same time have loved him diligently and will hopefully
die with these warm feelings. She turned and walked over to
Judith saying, "If you must spend your life loathing me, then
you must. Leave me now! She demanded.

"Take your wife home and love her as you always have. I shall
always love you as you have taught me."

The klonopin and beer was working, the tremors were gone. They
were gone. She made another phone call – calling her husband to
come for her. She was tired and the book was not going very well.

Several years quickly passed, and she was now 40 and he 72.
She sat at her computer, book still unfinished, responding eagerly
to the message strumming from her heart:

I think of you often I must say and where I might have been

If you had not come along my unforgotten friend,

to me, it is known the fact is clear, the struggle, still I face no one will ever come along and my time will you erase.

For several years you pulled me through the cracks and crevices with goal in mind for me to have the things I might have missed.

For more than the necessary things the hierarchy we climbed.

The task was clear the search was on a better life to find.

Your tender touch that meant so much guidance without control.

Now, no one's here my gentle dear to even play your role.

What wouldn't I do to speak with you, your hand reachout and hold?

Yet, I have been good; my ground I have stood and done as I was told.

Although summers aren't the same, my winters bring no pain.

I walk about day in and out feeling rather strange.

There is a part of me that is gone, to not have anymore.

But ah' the memories are mine forever to adore…

Betrayal

She was old but not alone and had not been alone since she first noticed that bear at her door. This morning was not unlike any other. As she took her usual stroll through her garden, the appearance of every flower and their aroma only recaptured the presence of daisies. The one flower she loathed; for, it reminded her of her best friend whose death was a mystery to most but a secretly lived nightmare to her.

The last 40 years of her life was filled with agony and fear. Agony from having taken the life of the oneperson whom she had shared her deepest secrets and dreams and fear of being discovered and exposed to the ones whom she had so selfishly tried to protect.

Her daughter, Pearl, was 41 now and had blessed her with three grandchildren. Justine, her adopted daughter, was 40 and had chosen to not have children or even a male companion, though quietly kept.

It was midday now and in the spring of the year. Yet, the beauty of the season offered no pleasure. The chirping of the birds was not amusing. Her inherited wealth with all its benefits presented itself without joy or comfort.

Deliliah entered the mansion and stared flatly at its artistic design. A servant approached her and asked, "May I get you something ma'am?"

"The usual," she dryly replied. He quickly returned with a fifth of Seagram's gin, lemon juice, and a bucket of ice, then asked, "May I get you something to eat ma'am?"

"Did I ask you to get me something to eat." She blunted

responded without a show of feelings. "You may be excused," she added.

She poured herself a drink and sat at a window near the east end of the house, where the scenery was bland with very little to appreciate. It somehow seemed the most fitting place for her. After a glass of gin, her affect and mood seemed less strained. Deliliah looked in the mirror only to see herself as the 30-year-old woman who had acted out unforgivably in rage caused by pain. I'm 70, but how is it I look so young.

Another glass of gin, and she looked in the mirror still seeing herself as a 30-year-old woman. This time she floated back to the night, 40 years ago when she was so happy and in love. When Pearl was only one years old, and Naomi had recently given birth to Justine. That night was supposed to have been a special night, and special it was.Justine was three months old. Delilah had managed to talkher best friend into spending the weekend in the cottage with she and her husband Rick. Naomi never went out andhad virtually lived with them since she'd gotten raped and discovered that she was pregnant for the rapist.

Deliliah was a nurse and worked the midnight shift. She asked Naomi to move in with them out of friendship and love, but Naomi quickly refused saying,"Girl, I can't impose on you like that I would just be in the way, I'm sure you'd get tired of me." But Deliliah reassured her it would work in the best interest of all concerned.

Nothing would give me greater pleasure than having my best friend here in the house with me to help look after my husband and child," she said.

"You need to think this over a little," Rick teasingly interjected.

"Aren't you a little bit afraid of having this beautiful 26-year-old rich white girl in your house alone at night with your handsome, flirtatious husband?

"Not a bit," Deliliah proudly swore.

Now as she sat there finishing up her third glass of gin,biting down on her lip trying to make the tears fall, hindsight ripped at her spine. Bitter bouts of agonizing memories continuously focused themselves as her past became her presence.

She quickly sipped down her fourth drink in her usual attempt to drown out the memories. This failed her. As she looked in the mirror, she again saw herself as the 30-year-old woman in bed with her handsome, husband making wild passionate love, swearing to him that she would do anything he asked her to do. After he made her scream, swear, and beg, she relaxed in his arms.

Deliliah, did you mean it when you said you would do anything I asked you to do?

"Yes." I wonder what this silly nut's up to now, she chuckled.

"No, no, I'm not even going to ask that of you.

You're enough woman for me," he said, while holding her close, caressing her butt."

"Rick!" she exclaimed, jumping from his arms, "you're not about to ask me if it's okay for you to have an affair?

Are you?"

"I don't know baby. We've been married for five years. You know I love you. Yet, I find myself daydreaming about making love to another woman. Forgive me?"

"What other woman Rick? Who is she?"

"Honey, there is no other woman, just fantasy." He reached over and covered her pubic area with his hand, "and I know I'm about to wear this good stuff out."

"Stop it, you silly nut. You're making my love jones come back."

Come to papa my little junkie and let me give you your royal fix." He started kissing her not omitting any sensitive part of her body until she reached her peak and rolledover in his arms still trembling from pleasure. Rick continued to thrill her as usual with his good old fashion stroking, until she became limp in his arms and begged him to stop.

"Just tell me what you want me to do," she begged, trembling at his side.

"Naomi," he mumbled. "I would really like to sleep with Naomi you know a menage - a trois."

"What!" she screamed, freeing herself from his embrace. Naomi, Naomi is like a little sister to me, and besides that she hasn't slept with anyone since she was raped. Every time I bring the subject up, she looks embarrassed and nervous. You know like when she had to tell us that her parents wouldn't accept Justine simply because she was half black. She never even told them she had been raped. No, we can't even talk about sex. She's so modest she'd probably flip out if I so much as suggested that to her. I'd hate to do anything to harm our relationship.

Nudging him in the side she confidently reminded him, "Rick, you know how much respect she has for me."

"Hell baby, I'm just worried about her. We have got to get her out of that shell. Just talk her into going to the cottage with us for the weekend, we'll have some champagne, soft music, blaze up the fireplace, and slip into something sexy," he said, pinching her on the butt, "you know how you love playing with the kinky hair on my chest, maybe you could just rub it a little bit and we won't have to talk about sex. Let's just seduce her. The girl needs to be made love to she's just scared.

Don't you want to help her out, just this one time?" Come on my adventure queen, let's free her, show her what good sex is really like. I'd enjoy making both of you sing the Campbell soup song."

"You are so crazy, just silly as hell," She giggled. "You really want to do that?"

He laid his head in her lap looking up at her like a mischievous little boy and said, "please baby, just this onetime then I will be fantasy free. Naomi will be frigid free, and you will forever reign as my queen."

"Okay, okay," she grinned, as he kissed her from her thighs downward. "But just this one time, you hear me, only once."

Who's the silly nut now, she wondered, while drinking down her sixth glass of gin continuing with her mirror talk. She remembered three days passing – drawing closer to that weekend – still trying to find a way to approach Naomi, when Naomi pranced into the living room, poured herself a drink and declared, "Deliliah you have got to help me snap out of this, I'm bored lonely, and frustrated. I've got to have an outlet!"

"Well, it's about time precious, why don't you, Rick and I spend the weekend in the cottage to sort of plan your coming out party?"

"You mean you would do that for me?" Some things are just too good to be trailed, after all how could anyone follow an act like yours big sis?" Naomi asked hugging Deliliah.

For the next two days Deliliah enjoyed the feel of mischief, being partly in control of the situation. After all it couldn't happen without her. Her exciting secret exhibited itself in her total existence as the weekend drew near. Every move she made was full of pizazz. She purchased tasteful provocative clothing, treated herself to a manicure, pedicure, facial. Had her thick black coarse hair styled in a twirl atop her head with a few strings hanging on her back and shoulders. Her posture became erect, and the swaying of her hips were as natural as the metamorphosis of a caterpillar.

Deliliah sat smiling into the mirror reaching for another glass of gin hoping to prolong that memory. Suddenly she heard this shouting sound coming from a nearby window. She walked over and opened it, seeing an angry Naomi screaming words that were not audible.

Staring out the window and pointing her finger at the figure dancing about in her conscious imagination," she drunkenly giggled but only for a second, the humor was quickly snatched away from her as she was drawn to the mirror and her glass.

Now sitting in her bedroom at the vanity, forty years earlier, looking sexy and feeling most confident while listening to the gurgling sounds prancing from the infant monitor that only moments before had been installed, what she heard caused a pain of such excruciating intensity that she begged God, "please let me die fast!" But death did not come, and Deliliah was left sitting paralyzed hearing a most torturous revelation, from Naomi and Rick as they entered the child's room.

"My, my, you have a lovely daughter her Missy," Rick teased.

"We do have a lovely daughter, don't we?" Naomi giggled.

"Hold me, kiss me, Rick, I just love you so much."

"I love you too much, Rick responded, holding and kissing Naomi.

"She looks just like you. How can Deliliah be so blind? Does she know that Justine is your child? Can she not see my face flush or my body tremble whenever you're around?" What about this gleam in my eyes that you put there or the pounding of my heart with my every effort to restrain myself and not reach out and grab you?

Does she not know? And" ambivalently she continued,"I love her so much, but I've just got to have you."

"I know Missy, and I love you too. But you know I love myself some Deliliah; let's just enjoy this for as long as wecan and when the time comes for us to pay… and hurt, perhaps we can remember the pleasure we found in loving each other."

"Well, that might not be much longer, especially after tonight. Deliliah is bound to pick up on something when you start making love to me and I start my praying and thanking Jesus, making all those promises to be good," she sheepishly chuckled.

"Hey missy, did I ever tell you about Deliliah's birthday?" he grinned.

Oh, no, here we go again, April 1," she giggled, "You so goddamn crazy." But I've decided to take my sleeping pills along just in case, maybe drop a few in her drink when things get hot and heavy so she'll go to sleep and we… my man… can freely express our love and lust," she brazenly interjected.

"I love you too much," he said, snugly holding her to his chest.

"But not as much as I love you," she melted.

The shattering sound from the bottle of gin against the mirror momentarily removed Deliliah from her atrocious state and she found herself back at the open window entering yet another inescapable hallucination.

"You had no right to eves drop on us, no right to kill us and take our child!" the voice shrieked at her.

Deliliah howled back, "My husband's daughter is just fine Wendy. A good little 'she-he' she turned out to be. Don't have to worry about her destroying a happy home due to bad genes.

Suppose you can say I've added new meaning to the word 'mammy flapper.' How do you like me now? Greetings to Casper.

You dare speak of rights? Certainly, you have rights now. It was you who had no rights then. Lies and hypocrisy lead you to your death. You lied about getting raped, slept with my husband, had his child, lived in my house under the pretense of being my friend.

Yes, now you have a right. A right to no longer exist. Every chance I get I go down the bee trail and spit on your grave!" As she turned around there stood a man and two female servants staring at her.

"Just what the hell do you all want?" she snarled.

"May I get you something?" the man servant asked.

"Don't tell me you don't know what you can get me, if you don't know by now, why you have got to be the biggest imbecile I have ever met," she laughed.

The man servant returned with a fresh bottle of Seagram's and her usual set up. "Thank you and leave me now!" she demanded.

She didn't have anything particular in mind. She wanted someone to hurt like her. There was a remorse like feeling swelling up inside her as she held her best friend in her arms. But no sounds came. There was nothing else to say, for a corpse cannot speak. The girl was dead. The husband was dead, daisies danced atop their graves. Love itself had not saved them for they had crossed the barrier of trust when they entered the world of lust. The true world of addiction.

There was never a question of whether Deliliah loved Naomi or Naomi loved Deliliah for it was well noted that they were close friends. Yet for some reason this day Deliliah held Naomi in her arms and lovingly rocked her as if no other day would come.

Malcolm

Daddy grabbed me by my shoulders and bending down looking me in the eyes ordered me to stay close to him and do everything he told me to do immediately.

"No damn time for hesitating!" He spoke.

Just this morning as I walked the fields beside him, he seemed like the biggest most compassionate person ever born. There was not a man, woman, nor child that lived on Mr. Charlie's plantation who did not adore my father. He was always in charge and Mr. Charlie was always satisfied at the end of the day. Even the field hands seemed to be content.

But now I'm frightened as I look into his glassy glaring eyes while constantly moving about, thrashing his arms in the air as if he were trying to shake something off his body, grabbing all the white man's guns from his cellar, hitting his head with his fists as if to keep himself awake. His face looked like a mask with a kinda blunted dull fixation.

The man appeared much older than his 30 years, his hair seemed to be graying and on edge. Even the lean frame of 5'10' 160 lbs., seemed monstrous like.

"Daddy what's wrong, what's happening?"

"Hush child, no time for talking," he said, steady loading gun after gun.

"Oh my God, the sheets are coming, right daddy those old sheets are coming after us."

"Don't you worry about a thang little honey bun, not a thang – naw' the sheets ain't coming after us. The sheets ain't coming at all."

"Well, what else could it be?" The day had been good. This morning daddy and I went out to the field, Malcom cried because he couldn't come. Five-year-olds were not allowed in the fields. Mama fixed him a lunch anyway and told him he could play with his little white friend, Jacob, from the big house. Malcolm liked playing with him. They were born a week apart and had played together all their lives.

"Okay, little missy, these guns are going on the wheel barrel and the rounds are going on the little wagon. Now daddy need you to pull the wagon and keep up to me little missy you got that?"

He knew I could keep up to him, every day out in the fields six days a week. I'm always at his side. The other children stand behind their parents but not me, I'm always at his side 'cept when mama need me. She six months in the family way now so she needs me a lot.

"This 1930 now honey bun folks ain't gotta take no shit – they just ain't gotta take no shit."

Daddy was crying, I never saw daddy cry before. I need to get to mama. "Daddy let's just go home to mama and Malcolm – everything will be all right, I'm scared," too scared to tremble in fact.

"Everything will never be all right again!" he roared, his body shaking as if it were being controlled by a tornado that didn't quite know what to do with him. His eyes protruding just waiting for one sneeze to send them bursting out of their sockets, boiling sweat popping off his body.

I know he has gone crazy but what can I do? Just got to get him home to mama; she'll fix him. It's three o'clock all the white men up at the big house outside in the shade sitting around that big ten-foot-tall red brick fence daddy and some of the other men build last week for this big dinner they are having today. Some secret dinner I guess 'cause they even got white folks to serve it, nope, no colored allowed.

Daddy wiped his face with a rag took a deep breath and the angry and painful, look left, his affect became fixed once again with that dull blunted appearance. We walked on toward the stable. He went out back to the pigs and fed them seeming somber in motion. I hadn't seen mama since noon when I went home for lunch and found out that Malcolm had beat up on Jacob, I went, "yea Malcolm." That was the first time Malcolm had ever hit Jacob back.

Most always Jacob would send Malcolm home crying with a fat lip or a lump upside his head and mama would just kiss that old lump or fat lip and say, "Malcolm, I just guess you go let your little blonde-haired, blue-eyed friend beat your brains out huh?" Then she'd hug and kiss him and send him back out there to Jacob.

Today was different and I was proud of Malcolm for putting a little knot upside Jacobs head for a sweet change. "Daddy it's about four o'clock, don't you think we should be getting home to check on mama? Mrs. Ann was over visiting her when I was home; she looked upset over Malcolm hitting Jacob back for a change; she was trying to get mama to whip Malcolm when I left and I'm kinda' worried about her."

"They gonna' have a dinner party of about 28 white men and about 13 women and a few children at five o'clock, then we'll leave."

"What does that have to do with anything? And I just know you ain't going to no dinner party with those old red neck crackers. I want to check on mama!" His affect became angry, and pain filled again. Tears mounted up in his eyes. Still, he stared me in my face, tears never falling.

"Baby gal" he said, "your mama refused to whip little Malcolm then asked Mrs. Ann out of the house when she insisted. She left and brought back Mr. Charlie, well you know Mr. Charlie couldn't make your mama whip Malcolm 'cause she's like that head strong and all, righteous, and God knows she loves herself some Malcolm," he said, half-laughing half not.

"Well Charlie started to hit her, but you know the woman didn't flinch. Saddie told me this. Yeah, Saddie was there til Charlie sent her out to the fields to get me 'cause he had some other work for me to do, I figure he just mad at me because he couldn't get my wife to mind him so's um go give him a little trouble in front of his friends cause if my wife is so strong then ain't I suppose to be strong too?

So, Charlie says to me, "Jesse, I got a cow and two calves outback that I want you to bury."

So, I say, "No sir Mr. Charlie can't do it right now just getting everything squared away out in the field give me about an hour or two and I'll jump right on it."

So, here stands Charlie with about 30 white men staring at me. He says, "Jesse you go bury this cow and these two calves right now," and reaches a shovel to me.

I said, "yes Sir Mr. Charlie, yes sir, you the boss man um' go do it right now," kinda' smiled and shook my head then walked out back behind the big barn all those crackers right behind me, "Where's the cow and calves," I say.

"Inside the barn Jesse, they inside the barn this time?"

I just laugh and walks on inside the barn – and Lord today, help me Jesus, there hanging up on some meat hooks is your mother cut open and a little baby girl hanging out – your little brother Malcolm right next to her with his throat cut, his wind pipe snatched out and both of his little hands cut off. I fell on my knees and prayed to God to please let me die fast! But he wouldn't.

Probably I would have died but um go tell you something about hate baby girl – hate kills by making the host stay alive long enough to plunge the dagger. When I looked up into the faces of those white folk about 40 of um not one set of eyes held compassion or remorse. Just read, we hope you learned your lesson nigger and tell all the others how we feel and what we are prepared to do."

He looked like he was in a trance and his bitter bouts of agony were well concealed as he clearly spoke on; there was no stopping him, even though I sat with my hands over my ears screaming, "no! no! For God's sake no daddy," paralyzed with pain.

"Baby girl you know I have some friends. Folks just like me, like they did your mama, but I ain't told a soul about this war but you. Cause we going to that dinner party and when they all sitting out there on the lawn around the dinner table safely locked in by that brick fence and praying to God to bless them, we go blast them to smithereens. Then we go, go and bury your mother, Malcolm, and your little sister.

Make comments @

https://meredithetc.com/no-recipe-intended/

Thank You

The End.

ABOUT THE AUTHOR

Shirley Francis, a Florida writer and published poet, was born in Covington County Alabama and raised in Pensacola, Florida where she presently resides. She is a Vietnam era veteran with four years of active duty in the United States Air Force as an aeromedical evacuation specialist. She was the first female to be Qualified on all three aircrafts the C-9, the C141 and the C130. She attended San Francisco Community College and completed the nursing program at Pensacola Junior College. She was formerly a medical surgical nurse and psychiatry nurse. She is divorced with three sons, nine grandchildren, and six great grandchildren.

https://meredithetc.com/no-recipe-intended/